Our Interwoven Lives
with the Zapotec Weavers

AN ODYSSEY OF THE HEART

BY SUSANNA STARR

PHOTOGRAPHS
BY JOHN LAMKIN

Paloma Blanca Press
Taos, New Mexico USA

Paloma Blanca Press
info@palomablancapress.com
877-520-4890
PO Box 1751, Taos, NM 87571 USA
www.PalomaBlancaPress.com

Publisher's Cataloging-in-Publication

Starr, Susanna.
    Our interwoven lives with the Zapotec weavers : an odyssey of the heart / Susanna Starr ; photographs by John Lamkin. -- First edition.
      pages cm
      LCCN 2013920484
      ISBN 978-0-9910956-0-5 (hardcover)
      ISBN 978-0-9910956-1-2 (pbk.)

    1. Starr, Susanna. 2. Zapotec weavers—Mexico—Teotitlan de Valle. 3. Businesswomen—New Mexico—Taos—Biography. 4. Zapotec Indians—Social life and customs. I. Title.

F1221.Z3S73 2013   746.1'4'097274

Cover & Book Design by Cowgirls Design • Taos
Cover Photographs by John Lamkin
Printed in the United States of America
First edition
19 18 17 16 15 14 8 7 6 5 4 3 2 1
Printed on acid free paper

*This book is dedicated
to the weavers of Teotitlan del Valle,
Oaxaca, Mexico and their families.*

*I hope this story serves as a reminder that business is
not a negative word. Trading is as old as human history,
whether for goods or services. It doesn't have to be
exploitative nor impersonal to be successful. Rather,
if it is infused with joy and happiness, it can provide a
vital, important and enriching aspect of our lives.*

Susanna Starr

INTRODUCTION

For a long time I've been encouraged to write about the years I've spent working with the weavers of a small Zapotec village high up in the mountains outside of the city of Oaxaca, Mexico. Not only have I had this encouragement from family, friends, and people I've dealt with through my weaving gallery in Taos, New Mexico over the past forty years but, most importantly, I've been encouraged by the weavers themselves.

Now the time has come to tell that story. Far from being a story of running a business of introducing and selling these weavings in the United States, this is a story of the personal interactions that have taken place between me and the Zapotec people of this village over the past four decades. The gallery that I've run during this time has simply been a vehicle

Opposite: *Iglesia* (church) in Teotitlan del Valle

to promote and distribute this particular art form. In the evolution of the gallery and of the weavings in general, as in any other part of life, many changes have taken place. But, as in any other endeavor, some constants remain.

For me the most important of these constants is the deeply personal connection I've had with particular weaving families as well as with the village as a whole. This connection has encompassed half of my life and the passion remains. Obviously, this is a personal narrative, but it also tells the story of people working together to preserve a culture and to promote a craft that has great impact not only on the individual weavers but on the whole village. The success I've enjoyed is mirrored in the success of that village and the individual weavers with whom I've been connected.

The story begins with my first visit in 1974, with my partner Ramon. Leaving the city of Oaxaca we headed toward the small weaving village I had heard about while still in Taos, New Mexico. We drove down a long, dirt road which took us through a somewhat hostile village whose inhabitants were resentful of the people of the neighboring village and refused to give any helpful directions. But, continuing on, we eventually reached our destination. We finally arrived at the small square that was the center of Teotitlan del Valle.

This book is divided into sections representing family generations. The first generation deals with that arrival and my initial introduction to the weavings. It paints a picture of the early years. There is a description of my own life at that time as well as my involvement with the Zapotec people of the village which was to become life changing for me.

The second generation is my work with the children of those initial weavers, after having had a long relationship with their parents. This is the same generation as that of my own three children. All of these children are now grown and well into the middle stage of their own lives. Although I am still very much connected to the parents, most of my business dealings over the past two decades have been with this second generation, children when I first knew them, and now associates in the business of collaborating on rug designs and choosing the weavings we would market.

The third generation, who are primarily teenagers and young adults, is now just coming into its own. Once again, there's the parallel with my own family. In this section we look at the grandchildren who have been raised in the weaving tradition but who have been afforded opportunities their own parents, and certainly their grandparents, were unable to enjoy when they were of a similar age.

In this time of instant communications and cutting-edge advances in the promotion of products, from smart phones to purchasing online, this narrative illustrates the fundamental exchange, on a very personal level, of real people and the weavings they produce completely by hand. Every weaving I've ever handled is infused with spirit. I know this to be a fact. It's not only the spirituality of the people that permeates all that they do, but also the authenticity with which they do it. Each weaving represents part of someone's life. No weaving machines or equipment of any kind are used, despite the availability of mechanized looms and computerized design.

This is not to suggest that the village is backward or unaware of changes that have taken place in the marketplace. Rather, they have chosen to incorporate many aspects of our contemporary world, while at the same time maintaining the integrity of their traditional way of life. But this third generation, as a result of the work and dedication of their parents and grand-parents, has been afforded many more opportunities to make different life choices. They have not only had the same exposure to the same things my own grandchildren have, but they have also had educational opportunities the previous generations had been denied.

The weavers I first encountered had only an early grade-school education in the village which was all that was available to them at that time. This second generation saw their children attend a newly built middle school. The third generation now has had access to high schools and universities. Weaving is still an option and a good choice for many of this youngest generation but for some, as you will see, their lives are taking different directions. Some things, however, remain the same, among them the sanctity of the family and the continuing importance of their cultural heritage.

Natural dyed yarns with cochineal and other organic materials

FIRST GENERATION

W e all have metaphors for events in our lives, including those that serve as markers. Some speak of beads strung together, one following the other, forming a chain of events or experiences. My favorite life metaphor is a tapestry. Only in my case it's literal as well as figurative.

This story begins in the summer of 1973 when I was living with my three children in the mountains of northern New Mexico fronted by a running river, surrounded by trees and bordered by national forest. I had often walked along the riverbank with my children and knew that a woman who was a weaver was living in a house close by. When I finally met her and we talked, I learned for the first time about an extraordinary weaving village she knew of in Mexico. As a weaver herself, she was rapturous in her praise.

Opposite: In the early days we frequently encountered
horse-drawn wagons on the road

I was especially interested because my family and I had just returned from an extensive stay in Mexico and I had fallen in love with the country and its culture. The mention of a relatively undiscovered weaving village in Mexico resonated deeply within me and I filed it away in the back of my mind. I was very interested in textiles and crafts, having opened the first crafts gallery of its kind in my suburban Long Island home several years earlier and having set up craft exhibits at places like The Parrish Art Museum in the well known artists' community of Southampton on Long Island.

In 1972 my husband Ian and I decided to leave the only life we had known together, sell everything we owned, and "hit the road." We bought a cab-over camper, packed ourselves and our three children into it, and wended our way from New York down to Florida to visit our parents, before crossing the Gulf Coast and entering Mexico through Texas. From there it was down to the Yucatan Peninsula, which was little known to both Americans and Mexican nationals at the time. Upon our return to the U.S. six months later, we explored the west coast of California but found it not to our liking. In one of those campground conversations that turned out to be life changing, we decided to return to the magical town of Taos, New Mexico where we had stopped briefly on the long trip northward from Mexico.

Shortly after our arrival there, my husband went back to New York for the summer to take care of several things while I remained at the campground with the rest of the family. The kids and I became involved with the alternative school that they would be attending that fall, a school that became an important part of our new community.

It wasn't until the following year, though, that thoughts of the small Zapotec village resurfaced. Meanwhile, my family had gone through the upheaval of separation and divorce. Although Ian continued to live close by, I was now living with Ramon in a new relationship that had begun in the Yucatan Peninsula. Both of us had felt a strong attachment not only to that area, but to all of Mexico. It was when we went back to Mexico together that we first explored this village, whose name of Teotitlan del Valle had never left my mind. We were not only exploring a new relationship but a way that would enable us to live in Mexico some of the time.

Driving to Mexico in 1974 was no easy task. Roads were narrow and traffic was horrendously slow, especially on mountainous roads behind the never-ending lines of old exhaust-spewing trucks lumbering up the steep hills. Many of the roads had no guard rails, which was especially nerve-wracking when you looked down a drop of several hundred feet. But most memorable were the ubiquitous potholes and flat tires.

There was always the sense that something worse could happen around any bend in the road. Twilight was especially challenging because of people walking along the sides of the road often carrying the day's load of firewood on their backs or riding bicycles without head lights or tail lights. Of course, there were always animals, like horses or donkeys, to look out for as well. Often, despite our best intentions to stop earlier, we drove well past dark, looking for a place to spend the night after the day's long and exhausting drive.

Finally, upon reaching Oaxaca in the south central mountains, we parked ourselves outside what was then a relatively small city and spent a day or two getting settled before setting out to explore the weaving village about an hour's drive away. When we finally arrived, driving through the long and narrow dirt road, we found ourselves in a small village of adobe houses flanked by a background of mountains. After a quick look around, we made our way to the central plaza where many weavings were displayed.

At the small market there, we stopped off at one of the stalls and spoke to the owner, a weaver whose display we liked. Explaining that we had no money but traveler's checks, he smiled broadly, assured us that there was "*no problema*" and informed us that he'd be happy to take our traveler's checks for the sampling of weavings we were to buy. Little did we know that this brief encounter would have such an impact and change all of our lives so dramatically. We were all — Ramon and I and the village itself — on the cusp of important change. It was one of life's memorable intersections.

The village of Teotitlan del Valle has been continuously inhabited by a group of Zapotec people for several thousand years, with many of their temples, such as the ones in the nearby village of Mitla, left well intact. Ancient carvings stand out in bas-relief, illustrating the source for many of the designs found today in the weaving motifs. Under the façade of the present church built by the Spanish on the previous site of the Zapotec temple in Teotitlan del Valle, one can see evidence of these beautiful geometric forms preserved under the overlying surface of plaster veneer.

Although the Zapotec people in this village had been weaving for centuries with materials available to them such as sisal, cotton, and rabbit hair, it wasn't until the arrival of the Spanish conquistadores and the sheep they brought with

Iglesia (church) sitting atop the ancient Zapotec temple ruins in Teotitlan del Valle

Ancient temple of Mitla showing the geometric patterns that have been and still remain the source for many of the motifs of the Zapotec weavings

Skeins of hand-spun Churro wool presently used to produce the weavings on the double harness loom

them that wool could be employed. The Spanish settlers also introduced the European-style double-harness loom. In the same way as the Navajo in the southwestern part of what was to become the United States started weaving, the Zapotec people here learned to weave in the new way, producing primarily ponchos and blankets to ward off the chill of the mountain air. When they later started weaving rugs, they created mostly stylized designs, using the motifs they saw in their temples or created from legends. The colors were generally natural colors of grays, blacks, whites, and shades of brown, heavy feeling in appearance. When they were dyed, they used bright colors from chemical dyes also introduced by the Spanish.

It was into this scene that Ramon and I made our appearance. Along with several other *compradores* (buyers), we worked with a small group of weavers, making innovative suggestions while always respecting what they were already producing. There were looms in virtually every household, but gradually we found ourselves dealing with just a small core of families.

On our first visit we had no idea what we could do to market these beautifully made weavings. We just knew that we loved them. We loved the people and the culture, and we felt we could do something to introduce them to other people in the United States who had no notion of their existence. The first few pieces that I brought back were sold quickly to a weaving shop in nearby Arroyo Seco outside of Taos, where we were living. Not long after, we were offered an area in The Ice cream Parlor, a large space that had recently opened on the Taos Plaza. Taos had become our home. It was a fit.

Our small Mexican-type stall was an instant success, but when the Ice Cream Parlor underwent extensive renovations, we found ourselves without a satisfactory space. However, on our way to pick up a newspaper to scan for a possible new location, we saw that a place close to the Taos Inn was empty. This space had, for many years, housed the shop known as Martha of Taos which sold designer Taos-style clothing. Martha had just moved to a location next door, leaving her smaller space, with the Mexican-style courtyard as its entry, available. It was an old, authentic adobe structure that had been a private home when it was built in the 1800s. It was not only beautiful, but it had an extensive history. We were entranced and delighted with our good fortune to find it available. And, what's more, we could afford it!

Immediately we began fixing up the courtyard as the way we knew them to be in Mexico. After all, it was an old building, later to be certified an historic site, built in the style of the Mexican colonials. It was the perfect environment for us. Beginning in a small kiosk in the Ice Cream Parlor, La Unica Cosa was now officially launched in the space that would become its permanent home. The name, which many folks had trouble pronouncing, meant "the only thing." However, that was really a play on words, since it was part of a phrase with a different meaning "I would like to go to the movies, the only thing is, I don't have the money." Although a quirky name, still, it worked for us and that name stuck for thirty years.

Shifting away from other crafts we had previously purchased in other parts of Mexico such as black pottery, hammered tin, and embroidered clothing, we now, in our new space, found our direction and focused exclusively on the

Zapotec weavings from Oaxaca. Starting out in the two small rooms previously occupied by Martha of Taos, we soon found ourselves outgrowing the space. When the gallery next door became available, it tripled our size, adding much needed space. Eventually, when that building was offered for sale, we quickly purchased it.

Our willingness to take on projects outside of our financial comfort zone defined our business as well as our personal lives. Just before the fledgling La Unica Cosa was launched, we moved into our home in the next valley north of Taos. We thought it was beautiful. Little did we realize it was even more unfinished than it looked.

The first few winters were daunting. What we took to be a roof was really just a covered ceiling. The beautiful *vigas* (posts) supporting the structure were not sealed, leaving openings where they joined the adobe walls, hardly protection against the frigid Taos winters. The children came home from school, after trudging almost a mile uphill from the country bus stop, along dirt roads covered in snow. They learned how to build fires to keep warm. We had no running water inside the house and electricity in just parts of it. Our only heat was from inefficient old wood stoves. Everyone knew how to chop wood and carry water.

As challenging as our home life was, the weavers in the village outside of Oaxaca were living pretty much at the same level. They had only one main road, although after a few years a new one was created that bypassed the adjacent village. Electricity was available only at certain times and then not to the people living farther away from the center of town. Vehicles and indoor bathrooms were rare. We could easily identify with the villagers.

Oxen in front of weaver's home waiting to be hitched

Although we were selling weavings and spending more and more time in the village working with a number of families, we still were balancing the need to buy more and build the business with our need to make a more comfortable home in which to live. Electricity had come to the entire house but it took a number of years and several attempts at digging a well before we had running water. The things we had taken for granted in our previous life were now what we worked for to improve the new life we had chosen.

During those early years, we worked seven days a week while living in Taos, and then spent several months in Mexico each year, making several trips to be with the weavers for extended periods of time. Once again, the parallel was apparent: We could see some of the changes in their lives as they were taking place in our own. Changes were also happening in the whole village as more people like us were coming down to buy there and sell in the market we were all establishing in the United States. The weavers, too, were doing the juggling act of trying to grow their businesses while providing a better way of life for their families.

As time went by, some of the families there were able to replace their dirt floors with tile, the adobe walls with brick, the basic wood tables and chairs with hand-carved fine furniture. Those who had electricity were able to install indoor kitchens to supplement the outdoor ones where cooking was done in the traditional way, over wood fires. Now, many of the weavers were driving their own vehicles. Instead of just working on their own looms in their own homes, some of the weavers got far enough ahead to be able to afford to hire others to work for them, although they were still directly involved in weaving themselves.

Interior courtyard of Florentino & Eloisa's home complete with auto and abundant
flowering plants illustrating present day prosperity of the village

As they expanded their weaving operations, they increased their production to meet the increasing demand. La Unica Cosa was also expanding. From having the one small space to later incorporating the complete wing of the original building, we also had several other outlets. Our children were grown now and while they were attending the University of New Mexico in Albuquerque, we opened two shops there that they ran. Having visited the village and having an early exposure to the weavers and their families, it was easy for them to create successful small shops in Albuquerque to help support their university studies. It also resulted in our ability to buy more weavings from the village.

For a number of years we rented a small house on the outskirts of Oaxaca. It meant that we could indulge ourselves in acquiring all kinds of wonderful

artesanía (handicrafts) from the different regions of Oaxaca. Most important, it kept us in touch with the village and the weavers on a regular basis.

The city of Oaxaca was growing, too. When we first arrived, some of the weavers used to walk around the *zocalo* (main plaza) with their weavings over their shoulders, hoping for sales from the small population of visiting tourists. Sitting on the park benches, we often looked out of the corner of our eyes hoping for a glimpse of Don Juan, the Yaqui Indian hero made famous in the chronicles written by Carlos Castaneda. The very same zocalo was also made famous through "*Mornings in Oaxaca,*" the novel by D.H. Lawrence. There was no doubt that magic was in the air.

One year, when we were set up at a campground on Avenida Violetas on the outskirts of the city, we met Isaac Vasquez and Emiliano Mendoza from Teotitlan who were showing their work to the owner of the trailer park, who introduced them to us. It didn't take long for us to recognize that they were master weavers and to begin what was to become a long lasting relationship with them.

By this time we were ready to buy weavings not only to re-sell but to preserve what we knew were some of the most outstanding pieces produced in the village. It never started out as a collection, but in the decade of the eighties, we acquired many pieces that would never be done again, primarily fine weavings of complex pre-Columbian images inspired by the glyphs of ancient codices. And *don* Emiliano and *don* Isaac were the masters.

Opposite from left: Pre-Columbian image woven by master weaver Emiliano Mendoza;
Large Pre-Columbian image woven by Emiliano and Arnulfo Mendoza - *Photos courtesy of author*

We always purchased special pieces from Isaac Vasquez, who was now featured in many collections throughout the United States and Europe and we visited regularly at his home and *taller* (workshop). But, it was with the family of Emiliano Mendoza that we made close, personal ties. When we had the opportunity to acquire a 9.9 square foot piece depicting an intricately detailed Mesoamerican calendar woven by don Emiliano and his oldest son, Arnulfo, which had taken years to produce, we decided to purchase it. It was one of only two of its kind ever produced by them. We went on to buy many others including several beautiful tapestries by his daughter, Abigail Mendoza. Abigail was a master weaver, as was her brother, Arnulfo. In those days, few women did any weaving. I don't know of any other woman weaver who produced the quality and creativity she brought forth.

We also purchased from Arnulfo Mendoza several tapestries of his own original images. Arnulfo had attended the Bellas Artes School and was a protégé of Oaxaca artist, Francisco Toledo, himself a protégé of famed Oaxaca artist, Rufino Tamayo. From there Arnulfo attended school in Paris where he was exposed to sophisticated art from European culture and where he developed his own interpretations in a style never seen before in his village. A weaver of immense talent, he was also a major painter and was later acknowledged by the government of Japan, where he spent six months as artist in residence during the early 2000s.

Our connection with the family continued when we worked with Tomas Mendoza, Arnulfo's brother and a fine weaver in his own right. Tomas was helping us acquire a clothing collection for our nearby sister shop in Taos. That

Pre-Columbian image woven by master weaver
Isaac Vasquez - *Photo courtesy of author*

was the shop that accommodated all the beautiful crafts of Oaxaca that we couldn't handle at La Unica Cosa, but loved.

When Arnulfo married Canadian, Mary Jane Gagnier, we attended their three-day wedding in the village. The wedding was extravagant and began with lines of guests filing down the unpaved roads to the church. The church was filled with flowers and elaborate hand-made decorations and the ceremony was led by two different priests. Festivities continued at the Mendoza home and followed the traditional style representing hundreds of years of custom and tradition, including dancing with the presents. The heavy hardwood chest that was made by Mary Jane's father was a challenging dance partner as was the refrigerator, but the hand-blown glasses that we gave them were a little easier. Sometime during the celebration the women entered with intricately painted *jicaras* (gourds) filled with sweets and then knelt down in file along the handwoven *petates* (mats) before gracefully exiting at the appointed time. Speeches were made, bands played continuously, and fireworks lit the sky. it was an important and major event.

We also visited with them frequently at their beautifully restored Spanish Colonial residence on Avenida Alcala in Oaxaca where they lived and ran an outstanding gallery called La Mano Magica, featuring fine Oaxacan art and crafts of the region. They showed the work of a number of important Oaxacan artists and their art openings were always a major social event of the art scene. These occasions afforded me the opportunity to dress in my favorite ethnic clothing. In addition to the fine crafts of the area that were on sale at the gallery, these art openings provided a much needed outlet for many of the painters to have their work displayed.

Alicia Montaño preparing hot chocolate in her kitchen
at El Descanso Restaurant

During those early years it was mainly intrepid travelers who made their way to this mountainous region of Mexico. As a result, the culture of the indigenous people remained largely intact. In the village, just a handful of outside people visited, tour buses not yet having made their appearance. We were welcomed as buyers but, more importantly, we were accepted as friends. When we came down with our children, they were warmly received. For us, the connections made during this time would continue to grow and deepen.

The Montaño family had a perfect location. They were right in the center of the village on a corner just across from the grade school. It was at a crossroads intersection and highly visible and accessible. When our friends and weavers, Edmundo and Alicia Montaño. asked us what we thought about their opening a small restaurant, we endorsed the idea enthusiastically. We carried a toaster oven to them when they first opened. Years later the kitchen had expanded to meet the needs of more customers. It had a first-class commercial oven and range and large refrigerators housed in a spacious and modern commercial kitchen. The tables were set with colorful hand-woven tablecloths and hand-blown glasses. The village lacked a restaurant that could not only provide a much-needed service but could also showcase their weavings more publicly. They had begun slowly with Alicia working in the restaurant seven days a week, still raising her four small children at the same time.

We, too, were raising our children and also working seven days a week. For all of us, this seemed like the natural thing to do. Their children were growing up as were ours. Their business was expanding as was ours. And their way of life slowly became easier as did ours. Soon we all had indoor plumbing! The

Woman from near-by village in Teotitlan to help in
food preparations for fiesta

village, too, was beginning to improve with more roads being paved, more services available, more electricity provided, and more houses being upgraded. That meant that their success spilled over to the carpenters, plumbers, electricians, plasterers, and builders they employed.

Meanwhile, the village retained its own culture and celebrated the many fiestas and special occasions on a regular basis. Not only were there various saints' days, but there were weddings, coming-of-age celebrations, baptisms, and more. Someone was always throwing a party — a direct family member or *padrinos* (godparents), *tios* (aunts and uncles), *primos* (cousins), or any one of the extended family and neighbors. I loved attending them and seeing the joy and laughter that always accompanied these celebrations.

The cooking was an elaborate procedure, often involving women from an adjoining village helping with the preparations. Huge cauldrons of food — *guisados* (stews), *caldos* (soups), and various *moles* (sauces) — simmered over open fires. Mounds of *masa* (ground corn) were stacked by the *comales* (flat metal cooking plates) to turn out the freshly made tortillas cooked over adjacent fires. The food was abundant and so was the mescal and beer that flowed as freely as the *refrescos* (soft drinks).

One of the things I noticed early on was that the men actively participated in these fiestas, primarily serving what the women had prepared. Although the men and women often ate at separate tables, guests were always given a special place of honor along with close family. Everyone was included in elaborate meals that sometimes took weeks of advance preparation. Although Spanish was the official language, many of the older people spoke only Zapotec

Elderly woman at traditional spinning wheel

and of those who did speak Spanish, they also spoke their own Zapotec language.

During these early decades women had a particular place in the decision making. Although not as "out front" as the men were when it came to the business part of our transactions, they invariably were there observing the transaction and conferring with their husbands about prices, in Zapotec. Very few women were weavers then (Abigail Mendoza being an exception), but they were involved in some of the other activities like spinning and dyeing. With many children to take care of, and with all the cooking, cleaning, washing, and marketing activities that were part of their daily lives, there wasn't much time left for the often laborious task of working at the loom.

Older people were revered and I loved seeing young children upon arriving home from school enter the room and immediately walk over to the elders, bend over and kiss their hands. These older people always had a home even if their spouses had passed on. The *abuelas* (grandmas) helped with the household and often cared for the babies and young children while the *abuelos* (grandpas) were sometimes to be found sitting on the traditional three-legged stool carding wool. When we first met Felipe Gutierrez' father, he was seated on one of these stools carding wool by touch, a dignified man then in his nineties and almost blind, but still participating in the life of his family compound.

Virtually every family had a *milpa* (plot of farmland) that was allocated to the individual families. At certain times of the year, especially when the corn was ripe, many of the men were out working on their *milpas*, harvesting the

Zapotec woman displaying her variety
of lilies in the market

corn that would provide them with the *masa* for the giant tortillas that were freshly made every day. The women left early in the morning, wrapped in their *rebozos* (shawls) to go to the market for the day's purchases of produce. Chickens and turkeys were often raised in the homes, scratching around in the open courtyards.

Early-morning marketing also included buying fresh flowers for the altar that was part of every household. From the poorest families to the most affluent, flowers were always in evidence on the altars, along with candles, photos of saints and deceased relatives, and other meaningful objects. Their spiritual connection was part of their life, not apart from it. It was also common for the weavers to do business in the same room that housed the altar.

Visiting the weavers close to the center of town was relatively easy but searching out the homes of other weavers who lived on the outskirts was another thing. The village is hilly and the roads at that time were pretty basic. There were rocks and potholes to skirt and, during the rainy season, deep mud. Since there were few reference points, it was sometimes confusing to try to find someone's home. The houses were often separated by a common wall, if it wasn't an individual compound, and everything was made of adobe. Fortunately for us, we were used to traversing dirt roads and the adobe architecture was the same as in northern New Mexico where we lived.

Our own house in Taos was made of adobe, and we, too, lived on a dirt road up a hill, where we could see the whole valley of Arroyo Hondo. We were also used to people having animals such as horses, goats, chickens, and pigs in their yards. Even the mountains that were our backdrop were also part of the

Oranges and papayas at one of the
fruit-stands in the market

landscape of the village in Mexico. Although not like the Rockies, they still were reminiscent of the areas that surrounded us in Taos. In Mexico, however, there were no snow-covered peaks.

Although our lives in northern New Mexico were just beginning another chapter, the Zapotec weavers maintained a continuity that had existed for thousands of years. Still, with the advent of people like us, they were also feeling a shift. I like to think that the impact on the village from the interaction with *extranjeros* (outsiders) was a positive one, since I never saw any signs to the contrary. From the very beginning, the *negocios* (transactions) were conducted with mutual respect. It was understood that we would all benefit from working together.

That sense of respect for the weavers was not necessarily in evidence in the city of Oaxaca where the indigenous people from the villages were still part of a different class. When Zacarías and his wife met us at our hotel on the zocalo, as we had arranged, we received a phone call from the desk. In a condescending voice, the manager told us "some people" were there requesting to see us. We went down to the lobby to meet them.

Attired in their traditional dress, he wearing sandals and carrying a package and his wife in her traditional *huipil* (hand embroidered blouse) and *rebozo* (shawl), her braids entwined with ribbons, we welcomed them warmly. Later, when we had dinner in the dining room, it was even more of a surprise to the staff. When the check came, instead of allowing us to pay, this Zapotec weaver from the village took out his credit card and handed it to the waiter who looked amazed while Zacarías watched with a twinkle in his eye.

Specially adorned altar for Day of the Dead at
home of Alta Gracia, dyemaker

SECOND GENERATION

By the early 1990s we had made some of our most important and collectible rug purchases. The intricate pre-Columbian designs were rarely being made so we were grateful we had had enough foresight to get them when we could and preserve these important weavings. We put them away carefully, knowing that some day they would document some of the finest weavings ever produced in the village. Having them out in the world, appearing as one or two pieces that were purchased privately, wasn't the same as having a collection. It never started out that way, but during the eighties, we were able to make significant purchases. Not knowing what to do with them, it seemed that just having them in one place was part of our role to preserve an important

Two village woman at market in Teotitlan buying flowers
and candles to decorate their altars

part of the artistic history of these weavers – Emiliano Mendoza and Isaac Vasquez in particular.

Beyond the acquisition of these weavings, the eighties were significant for us in that the members of the second generation of weavers were now beginning to actively work with their parents and were taking over aspects of the businesses. Now in their twenties, they were getting married and starting families of their own. The custom in the village is that when a son gets married he brings his wife into his family. Obviously, the reverse is true when a daughter gets married and leaves to live with her new husband's family. Although there are variations on this theme, depending upon circumstances, this was pretty much the accepted form.

With the Montaños, Alicia and Edmundo, they broke even. Their son Pedro married Carina and their son Fidel married Marisela, bringing both young women into the family compound. Their daughter Antonia married Tommy and their daughter Alicia married Ismael and left to live with the families of their new husbands. It so happened that not only did their children marry within a few years of each other, but to a great extent married into the same family, exchanging not only young wives and husbands, but forging close ties through marriage with a specific family. Carina and

Pre-Columbian image of Maya
"Vision Serpent" – *Photo courtesy of author*

Marisela, who were cousins, lived in the Montaño family compound and helped significantly with the growing restaurant, while their husbands worked at the looms and dye pots.

This also meant that their children, who were actually cousins, were raised almost as brothers and sisters. They were carried around together as babies, they played together and they ate together in their grandparents' home. What closer family ties could be forged? Diana was the first grandchild, born to Pedro and Carina. The new grandparents, Edmundo and Alicia, were understandably ecstatic. A few years later, Pedro and Carina's son Diego was born. About the same time, Fidel and Marisela had their son, Fidel.

Alicia and Edmundo's vivacious daughter, Antonia, was also married and busy having children of her own. Soon after, the youngest daughter, Alicia, started her family. Both of the daughters visited the family compound almost daily, so all the little cousins were closely connected and mid-day meals often included everyone. For me rattling these names off is almost as automatic as naming my own children.

Most of the other original families we had been working with were at the same stage, with grown children having their own children. Things rolled along smoothly with no abrupt transitions. Rather, it was a natural, organic evolution with no one questioning their place in the world. Their place was established: working for and with their families. This was not true in all cases, however, especially with the weavers who were less financially successful. In these families, there were always a few brave souls who left for the U.S. to try to find work that would allow them to send money back to their families in the village and thereby improve their lives. Although some remained in the states, many returned to the village.

As sometimes happens, with time we became more disengaged with a number of the first families we had worked with. The core group was growing smaller, but each individual family was growing larger with the addition of the second-generation weavers under the same roof. In the Montaño household, Pedro and Carina had a third child, Alicia, and Fidel and Marisela had Sara. They were all so close that Sara called her aunt "mamá" and her mother "tia" (aunt). When we would jokingly ask her "Donde está tu mamá?" (Where is your mother?), she would point to her aunt with a perfectly serious face. When we asked her where her aunt was, she would point to her mother. Even at an early age, Sara was precocious and delighted in seeing everyone's response to her pronouncements.

In Felipe Gutierrez's family, his two sons, Armando and Juan, and later young Felipe, were also stepping into their places as the next generation of weavers. And, of course, they too were raising their own families. This progression was not only important for the continuity of the now established businesses, but it also allowed the first generation to step back a little from their years of hard work. Felipe began spending more time in the *milpa* (plot of land) working at the farming he loved, while Edmundo Montaño spent more time involved in sports.

This second generation also had more access to an education with the newly built *secundaria* (middle school). They soon were realizing the importance of speaking English with clients who didn't speak Spanish, which helped a lot in

Fidel Montaño with his daughter, Sara, and niece, Alicia, an early photo

their negotiations. They continued taking over the business end of their fathers' businesses, keeping ledgers of their various clients and dealing with them now as equals. Gradually, this second generation contributed their production of weavings to sell as well.

The village, itself, was also undergoing significant changes. During these years it became more affluent as the weavers grew their businesses, often employing many other weavers to work for them.

During the eighties, many advances were made under the two-year terms of elected officials known as *mayordomos* (mayors). Some of these included building a sports stadium, later adding lights so sports could be played at night, paving many more streets, beefing up the electricity so many more families could benefit, providing sanitation services, building the *secundaria*, expanding the curriculum of the schools (including study of their own Zapotec language), providing an expanded health clinic and a library, and establishing other important services designed to improve the life of all the villagers.

Home construction boomed and houses underwent expansion and upgrades, replacing adobe with brick, adding amenities as well as furnishings. All along the *entrada* (entry road), where no buildings had previously existed, spacious new homes were being built, including impressive showrooms fronting the road. Many of the established weavers purchased land along this entry into town with an eye to building future homes for their children. Rather than the cactus that had prevailed for generations, the new homes included extensive and beautiful landscaping. Luscious bougainvillea, cascading over walls, provided bright splashes of color everywhere. Where once the *entrada* was simply the entry

Felipe Gutierrez's son Juan showing one of his rugs

road into the village, it was now becoming developed with new homes constantly making their appearance. It was a great way for some of the weavers to have a more public space in which to attract clients as well as provide homes for their children.

This second generation was now being provided with opportunities and alternatives their parents never had. One of Isaac Vasquez's sons became a doctor, and when Isaac's granddaughter was offered the opportunity to study medicine, she weighed it carefully before deciding to be a weaver and marry and raise a family. One of Emiliano Mendoza's sons became an *abogado* (attorney) and his daughter, Abigail, opened Tlamanalli, the first gourmet Zapotec restaurant in the village. Working together with her sisters, the family built a world-class restaurant and gallery that's featured in all the guide books.

Our visits were always punctuated with reminiscing about the early years, passing on those memories to the children who were now adults. Our ties were real and meaningful, transcending just a business relationship. What we had was something fuller, richer, and based on familiarity and trust. And we always compared notes on our families.

Our own family was now grown, too. Although my oldest daughter had previously run a shop in Albuquerque during some of her college years, she was now ready for own career. She started an alternative high school and later started teaching at the University of New Mexico, where she became an adjunct professor in philosophy and world religions. She went on to become a published author and speaker. My youngest son was involved briefly in one of our galleries in Durango, Colorado, but since he had always been interested in

Felipe Gutierrez's son Armando at the loom

acting, that was just a temporary situation for him before he went to study theater in New York and then in Los Angeles, where he made his home.

Only my middle daughter who had run a shop with her husband in Albuquerque when she was at school, worked with us at the gallery in Taos. For a number of years we worked as a family of four, representing two generations. We also expanded not only our staff at our main gallery, but opened a number of other shops, as well. Our second shop in Taos gave me the pleasure of (or excuse for) buying more of the wonderful treasures we always encountered in Oaxaca.

Our main gallery sold only weavings, for which we were well known. There were brief forays into other locations, but Taos remained our home base. In addition to acquiring the collection of special weavings from the village, we also commissioned art pieces of images from some of the well-known artists in Taos such as R.C. Gorman, Jim Wagner, Charles Collins and Jonothan Sobol, for sale in our gallery in Taos.

We continued to build pretty much as the weavers were doing. Our home became more comfortable and more beautiful, although with working seven days a week, there wasn't much time to enjoy it. Wherever we found interesting pieces of sculpture, paintings, carvings, jewelry, or textiles, they found a place in our homes in Oaxaca or in Taos. Our connection between Oaxaca and Taos was evident in both our business life and in our home life.

Taos, too, was growing and becoming known as an art center, on a smaller and more limited scale than the well-known city of Santa Fe, New Mexico, just an hour and a half south. There had been a great reception to the weavings over the years, and we were still actively involved in introducing people to the Zapotec culture. We were also actively involved in working with the weavers on color and design direction, although we continued to buy from them their pieces that represented the very finest in Zapotec weavings.

It was during this time that we expanded our connection to the Yucatan Peninsula. In the mid-eighties, we decided that the area we had known in the northern part of the Peninsula for the past decade or more was rapidly changing because of the development of Cancun and the surrounding areas. We weren't happy about the inevitable growth that was on the verge of development. It was just a matter of time before all the little turnoffs to the beaches we knew so well were going to lead to areas of mega-resorts. The feeling of discovery that Ramon and I had enjoyed since the early seventies would soon be over.

With that in mind, we found ourselves receptive to the idea of moving not to a beach area on the magnificent Caribbean that we knew and loved so well, but farther south where there was virtually no development nor tourism. After years of sand in our beds, in our food, and in our clothing, we discovered magical Laguna Bacalar, several hours south and a little inland, close to the border with the country of Belize.

The universe not only presented us with a lovely home directly on the water, called the Lake of the Seven Colors by the ancient Maya, but the following day we also found a beautiful piece of undeveloped land just a few kilometers away. When faced with the decision of which one to act upon, we decided upon buying both. After struggling to make our home livable in the cold, snowy climate of

Taos, the idea of living in a finished home fronting tropical waters that looked like the Caribbean but were freshwater and calm rather than salty and often rough, was very appealing. Having the opportunity to landscape it was like frosting on the cake!

But for Ramon and me, just having a home was never our intention. Creating a special getaway where people could experience this part of the world that we so loved was a vision that had been planted in our brains when we first met in the Yucatan a dozen years earlier. At this point, we were able to do something about it. Our relationship with the weavers was now firmly established and we had an easy rhythm with them. This allowed us to withdraw some of our energy from the business in Taos and focus on creating something else on Laguna Bacalar, while still maintaining our strong connection with the weavers.

Each day we were there, during the several months we lived in Bacalar, we worked on first the house and then the creation of what was to become Rancho Encantado. It was exciting to see it all unfold. The adventures we had there will have to find their place in another chronicle, but it was the third piece in our particular trilogy. Our primary home was in Taos, surrounded by the presence of the Tewa people of the Taos Pueblo. Our second "place" was in Oaxaca where we were immersed in the culture of the Zapotec people. And our third was living in the land of the Maya in the Yucatan Peninsula of Mexico. Being in the physical presence of these three great indigenous cultures for so many decades has been a blessing in my life on many levels.

These were building years for the weavers as well as for us. We built the Rancho as we could, in spite of having little extra money and no experience and no concrete vision of what we wanted to see. But the project took on a life of its own and by the end of the decade of the eighties, we had created the first eco retreat/resort of its kind on the Yucatan Peninsula. All the people who worked with us were local and received on-the-job training, as did we.

We could now share some of the beauty we knew with others who wanted to come down to explore the incredible surrounding archeological sites in the area as well as experience the pristine waters of Laguna Bacalar, away from the madding crowd. It was a special place that afforded privacy and tranquility, and many visitors never did more than simply relax and enjoy the beauty and serenity of being there. And I, of course, could indulge in my favorite activity, landscaping. I had already completed that project at our home a few kilometers away and was ready to take on the larger project at Rancho Encantado.

Along with old-growth hardwood trees on the property were many coconut palms. After a couple of years of clearing the jungle growth and then gradually building the casitas, the new landscaping slowly became established. Bougainvillea and hibiscus were everywhere now, as well as fruit trees and ornamental plantings.

By the nineties Rancho Encantado was pretty much complete. We had thirteen casitas, two large *palapas* (thatched roofed, open-air structures), docks and walkways, staff housing, lawns and lots of tropical plants and trees. The dining room served beautiful and healthy food and we featured handmade crafts from Oaxaca in the *tienda* (shop). Now we could turn our attention once again to Oaxaca.

With the expansion of our primary gallery and other shops, we were now buying heavily. We were seeing results from the years of trying to promote Zapotec weavings and introduce people to the culture. Feeling well established and satisfied with what we were doing, we were unprepared for the next step, which required another significant decision and shift in what we were doing in the village, expanding our weaving horizon in a way we couldn't have imagined.

We received large shipments from the weavers on a regular basis from the various visits each year to the village where we were now making substantial purchases. They were stored in a *bodega* (warehouse) nearby in Taos. One day, some time in the late eighties, much to our surprise, we unpacked a shipment that we knew we hadn't purchased. They were completely different from anything we had ever seen and we loved them! We traced them to the person to whom the shipment was intended and found that he was someone we knew from both working in the village and, before that, from Taos.

After arranging to send this misdirected (by the delivery people, not the universe) shipment to the proper recipient, Richard Enzer, we also spoke with him about handling some of his production. Partially based on his background of being the director of an Oriental rug gallery in New York and partially with his experience in the same village we all were working in, Richard had come

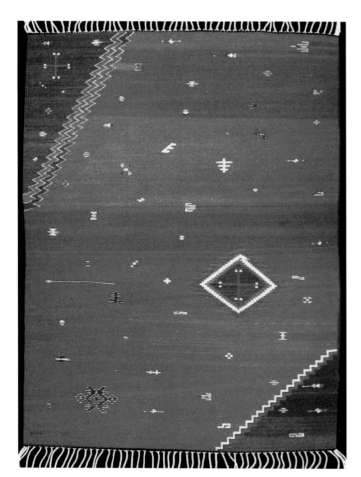 

From left: A weaving from the Line of the Spirit collection; "Nomadic" from the Line of the Spirit collection

Opposite page: "Hopi Ceremonial" from the Line of the Spirit collection

Photos courtesy of Starr Interiors

up with a collection that represented a fusion of various cultures. They not only carried elements from various weaving cultures including nomadic tribal design inspirations from the mid-east, but also carried design elements from areas in the southwest region of the United States, including Navajo, Zuni, and Hopi elements as well as some from the Plains Indians.

The stunning designs were further enhanced by the use of intense color. These colors were unique and not to be associated with what had previously come out of the village. They were deeply saturated, creating a vibrancy that was truly exciting. We later learned that Richard had spent a good deal of time working with a woman from the village, introducing her to the dyeing process he had learned from famed weaver and dye-maker, Rachel Brown, from Taos. Together with Sergio Martinez, a young and talented weaver from the village, they created a new line of weavings they called the Line of the Spirit.

This collection was produced by a carefully selected group of weavers who were shown the new patterns and the new use of the colors produced by the dye-maker, Alta Gracia. The yarns used were completely hand-prepared, starting with the fleece of the Churro sheep. Periodically, excursions were made to a small, remote village high in the mountains, reached by bumpy and winding dirt roads, where they specialized in hand-carding and spinning using the ancient and traditional drop spindle to produce individual balls of yarn.

This village seemed a throwback in time. The Churro sheep, introduced to this continent by the Spanish more than five hundred years ago, still thrived there. The people of this remote village of Chichicapam had never dealt with the outside world; they lived the way they had lived for centuries. Because of

Group of Line of the Spirit weavers in the
garden of dyemaker, Alta Gracia

the three rivers that ran through the village, their fields provided ample grassland for the sheep to graze, producing thick, luxurious fleeces.

In addition to the fine wool produced by the villagers, they had another claim to fame, mescal. As if the ride to this village wasn't enough, going from house to house, looking at the yarn, sampling the mescal was just as important. Each house took a special pride in the homemade brew they prepared in their backyard stills. It would have been impolite not to accept their hospitality. By the time we had made a number of stops, those of us who were drinkers (myself definitely not included) made the return trip down the mountain laden not only with wool, but with the bottles of mescal we had purchased. It was a party atmosphere. All the hours spent driving up those mountain roads and trudging in and out of the individual houses yielded a great haul; our old van filled with balls of handspun wool and a few bottles of mescal to take home.

After a couple of years of handling the Line of the Spirit with great success due to both the quality of the pieces and our own great enthusiasm for and appreciation of them, Richard called to set up an appointment to meet with us. He brought Sergio Martinez with him. Sergio was the art director, which

Recent photo of author, Susanna Starr with Richard Enzer, founder of the Line of the Spirit

basically meant that he was in charge of production. Richard also had a dye-maker, an office liaison person, and a number of carefully chosen weavers working on the Line of the Spirit. It was a great *equipo* (team).

Everything was in place, he said, for the collection to take off, but he needed a partner, and we were the ones selected. It seemed to be the natural choice. We were well known, established buyers and respected in the village and we loved the collection. So we agreed to enter into a partnership with him. We bought half of the business and worked together in the village, being introduced to a completely different group of weavers and, of course, to the dye maker, Alta Gracia.

Richard, the founder of the Line of the Spirit, was one of those people you sometimes meet along the way who seem to be "larger than life." On our first visit to the village after we had become partners, he assumed that we would be spending most of our time working together in the village. In this regard he was right. We spent many months trudging from one weaver's home to the next, standing by each loom, watching the exchange between Richard, Sergio, and each weaver.

The days were often hot and the village dusty. We started out in the morning and usually didn't return to the city until dark. It was thoroughly exhausting, but also exciting and interesting. Even with our own extensive background and experience, it was the deep daily immersion in the Line of the Spirit project that enabled us to learn it all from the first step of driving up to the wool village, having our arrival announced over the loudspeaker, and then choosing the handspun wool from the women who gathered in the town square in response to the announcement. From there, we took the wool back down to the weaving village, where it was spun into skeins and then readied for the dye pots. We participated in each step.

The dye making was done over an open fire and the colors produced were always amazing in their depth and vitality. Some of the intricate weavings took many months on the loom and some of the largest ones took nearly a year. A few of the weavers lived close to the center of town but many lived on the outskirts and were much more difficult to reach on the winding and bumpy dirt roads. All the weavers were excited about what they were doing and took great pride in working on the project and protecting the designs which were new and different. Their dedication was real.

But the other of Richard's assumptions, that we would live with him in Oaxaca during this initial period, never worked out. We were happy to be immersed in the work in the village, but we needed to have our own living space and privacy. Richard always had a retinue, much as a rock star. He had friends who were artists and musicians plus others who just liked to "hang out." His home was always a party scene. After our first visit, we knew immediately that we needed to find a place of our own. We needed more privacy and quiet time. The next morning found us sitting on the Zocalo with a newspaper scanning the homes for rent in the classified section.

One of the offers sounded just right and when I called the person, it sounded even better. We met the owners, Concha and Moises, at the house in a residential area just outside the city. It was small, but had a front *terraza* (terrace) and a garden area that I loved. We had our own car so the relatively short driving

Alta Gracia immersing the wool in her dye pot
over traditional wood fire

distance into town wasn't difficult. We rented it on the spot and moved into it later in the day. Richard agreed that it was a good choice and referred to it as the country house while his apartment in Oaxaca was the city house. It all worked.

Early in the morning we would set out to pick up Richard, then Miriam, our liaison person, at her house for the drive out to the village. Often we'd stop off along the way at Tule, famous for the enormous and ancient tree growing in the center of town, to have the large tortillas known as *tlayudas,* filled with corn, squash, or chicken, served with hot yellow sauce. There were many stalls in the market with women working at the various *comales,* cooking up *comida tipica* (traditional food), served with fresh squeezed orange juice or *aguas* (fruit drinks). Richard, of course, had his favorites. Although his Spanish was limited, his enthusiasm wasn't and with his friendly, jovial manner, he was welcomed everywhere.

Back in the city after the long working days, we needed no excuse to visit the outdoor cafes along the Zocalo or listen to music somewhere like El Sol y La Luna, and be with friends, like Mitzi Linn, Richard's "spiritual advisor." There were gallery openings, too, and we were always part of those gatherings. Just as the art scene was flourishing at this time in Taos, so it was in Oaxaca. Since we were in a different category than tourists but, rather, lived and worked there, we were part of a scene during the eighties and nineties that established us as *medio-Oaxacaños* (half Oaxacans). And it was, to an important extent, our home while we were there.

We filled our new little second home with beautiful weavings by our weaving families. From our artist friends and from new purchases at gallery openings, we

Famous centuries-old tree in the center of the nearby
Zapotec village of Tule

acquired paintings and sculpture. And from the various outlying villages, we purchased beautiful clay, tin, and wood pieces and, always, woven textiles. We had the traditional blue and white Oaxaca dishes and hand-blown glassware. Having a home there allowed us the indulgence of buying some wonderful crafts of the region. I had also acquired an outstanding collection of ethnic clothing, including an array of *rebozos (*shawls) that I wore regularly.

The state of Oaxaca has what is called the *"siete regiones"* (seven regions). Each of these regions is marked by a particular costume. Once familiar with them, you could recognize that region by the *huipiles* (blouses) and *faldas* (skirts) the women wore. Since their short stature is about the same as mine, it was easy for me to wear the clothes. I felt like famed Mexican artist and feminist icon, Frida Kahlo!

As fiestas were taking place in the city, there were also ongoing fiestas in the village. They were large, important occasions with extended families and

friends, vast quantities of food, traditional brass bands, lots of flowers, and plenty to drink. Attending them, we were always treated as honored guests. Although our relationship with the weavers was that of business, there was something between us that went deeper and was much more meaningful.

During the eighties and nineties, building these personal connections was the most important thing for us. They were connections built on mutual trust

Traditional huipiles from one of the seven regions of Oaxaca on display at a market

Opposite page: Stylized bird carving, hand painted from the village of Arrazola, famous for its production of *alebrijes*

and confidence that come from people knowing each other over time and expanding that relationship beyond that of just business associates, but of friendship based on mutual respect. This second generation, who knew us from our established relationship with their parents, now were the ones we were dealing with more and more.

Our Line of the Spirit team also changed when our wonderful friend Miriam left to study music in Mexico City. Now, another young woman, Abi, took her place. She became not only the new liaison but a friend, confidante, and quasi-family member for the next twenty years. As much as I loved her like a daughter as well as friend, so did the people of the village whom she loved also. Over the years of working closely, we laughed together, occasionally cried together, and injected continuing life into the Line of the Spirit connection. The other weavers we were dealing with also welcomed her into their homes. She was an enthusiastic participant in all we were involved in, as well as being the director of the Line of the Spirit project. When we would show up at the home of the dye maker, Alta Gracia, Abi would immediately make herself at home, picking fruit off the trees and enjoying the ubiquitous handmade tortillas hot off the *comal*. To everyone, she became family.

When, after twenty-two years of being together, Ramon and I parted ways, it was a tremendous surprise and shock to the weavers, as well as to me. We had spent these many years building our business in Taos, the eco-resort/retreat in the Yucatan Peninsula, and, the foundation for it all, our relationship with the weavers. I went down to Oaxaca alone for the first time in 1997. I think it was then that I realized the true depth of the feelings

Exchanging news at the morning market while
buying flowers for their altars

expressed by the weavers through their deep concern for me. Felipe could only shake his head in bewilderment that such a thing could come to pass, and Alicia, despite her best efforts at self-control, couldn't help the tears that ran down her face.

Later that year, it was with great relief and open hearts that they warmly welcomed my new partner, John, who accompanied me on the next trip down. Speaking Spanish and familiar with Mexico since his first trip there in the fifties, not to mention being able to join in the singing of traditional Spanish songs, made him immediately welcome. But the additional element of acceptance came from their feeling of relief that I was no longer alone and had a partner to share my life with.

Close-knit families are one of the most important characteristics of Zapotec culture. The first time John and I sat down to *comida* (main mid-afternoon meal of the day) with the Montaño family, John was given the full treatment. By now, one of these meals included not only all four of Alicia and Edmundo's grown children and their spouses, but also most of the grandchildren as well. It didn't take more than the first visit before John became *"tio Juan"* (uncle John).

In addition to the more traditional food of Oaxaca, the Montaño family could always be counted upon to serve lighter dishes, featuring fresh salads and lots of vegetables. With Abi accompanying us, it was expected we would all join the family for *comida,* the main meal of the day. We exchanged stories and heard the latest *chisme* (gossip). We always had this wonderful family meal together before we embarked on choosing the weavings we would buy.

Author, Susanna Starr, with Abigail Zarate going over
Line of the Spirit weavings

Zapotec traditional dishes at a market

Comida at El Descanso restaurant with the Montaños
Photo courtesy of Susanna Starr

By this time, not only the Montaños, but also other families were becoming more health conscious. Being involved in sports trimmed down a lot of the men. Less meat and more vegetables were gradually edging out the traditional *guisados* (stews) and the famous *moles* (seven different kinds of gravy sauces, sometimes made with chocolate). Luckily, the fabulous homemade soups were still very much in evidence, like *sopa de calabaza* (squash soup with squash flowers), *higado* (chicken soup with dumplings) and *sopa de tortilla* (tortilla soup).

Comida at the home of another weaving family, Florentino and Eloisa Gutierrez, was always a special occasion. Eating out in their large, sunny courtyard surrounded by flowering plants and vines provided the backdrop for many sumptuous meals. Eloisa is a superb cook, serving healthy and traditional Zapotec dishes as well as fresh vegetables. Abi has always been welcomed into their home, as with the Montaño family, as a good friend. And, as always, there's been fun and laughter and joy before we got to look at their weavings. There really is no separation of friendship and business so buying and discussing the weavings together is simply part of it, as is eating, telling jokes, and catching up on family activities.

Each year brought new advances. The labor-intensity of meals made from scratch was now being alleviated by new stoves and refrigerators. Tortillas, of course, were still made completely by hand, and every household had stacks prepared to throw on the *comal* to serve "hot off the press." The increase in the number of cars and trucks, cameras and computers, tile floors, and indoor plumbing was something welcomed by everyone who

Isabel Bautista making tortillas in outdoor kitchen

From left: Cross for Day of the Dead decorated with marigolds;
Day of the Dead celebrant dispensing mescal at parade in Mitla;

74

Day of the Dead floral offerings at the cemetery in Teotitlan

could afford them. There was a library and health center and more educational opportunities. But many things did not change, which was something for which to be grateful.

Holidays were still celebrated in the traditional way, and none was or is more important than the celebration known as *"los dias de los muertos."* Called in English "Day of the Dead," the celebration is actually two days, the first welcoming the spirits of departed children and the second welcoming the spirits of departed adults. The entire village prepares weeks in advance for this holy holiday. Every altar is decorated with flowers, candles, photos of the deceased, and other offerings. It culminates by a celebration in the cemetery, where people come in laden with flowers to place at the graves of their loved ones. Mescal and beer are passed around, and bands play for hours, creating

Delivering specially decorated Day of the Dead breads

Opposite page: Tradition skulls for Day of the Dead made of spun sugar displayed in theTeotitlan market; Band playing in front of the cemetery chapel

a party atmosphere. For the Zapotec people, as with many indigenous cultures, death is part of life and is celebrated as such.

A number of years ago we went to the cemetery along with throngs of people from the village who came to party there in honor of the *difuntos* (deceased). My daughter asked me to place at the altar of the chapel there a photo of her daughter, Jenny, who had been killed in an automobile accident some years earlier when she was just fourteen. If I had had a photo of my son, Matty, who died when he was ten and a half, I would have placed it there. Instead I lit a candle.

Although obviously all who were there mourned their loved ones, there was the prevailing atmosphere of a celebration, acknowledging death as part of life. Virtually everyone carried bouquets of flowers or carried beer or mescal with which to toast the departed, knowing that this was just a brief visit with them.

When Don Emiliano Mendoza passed away, his son, Arnulfo, painted a dancing skeleton in a richly textured visual interpretation of his feelings for his father. His death was during the same year as that of my own father, whom I adored all of my life. We ended up buying that painting honoring our fathers and it hangs even now in a special place in my Taos home. This was a decade of many shifts, the death of parents, the dissolution of my long-term relationship with my life partner, Ramon, the beginning of my new relationship with John, important changes in the village, and the growth and transformation of Rancho Encantado, our eco-resort/retreat in the Yucatan Peninsula of Mexico.

Author, Susanna Starr, placing photo of
granddaughter on altar in chapel at cemetery

Having three homes seemed like too much, now that we were spending less time in Oaxaca with the weavers and more time at the Rancho, so we gave up our little house on Calle Rafael Osuna in Oaxaca and concentrated on creating a special place where groups could come and enjoy the spiritual renewal of Laguna Bacalar at Rancho Encantado in the Yucatan Peninsula. The groups that came were wonderful and the bonding that took place was special. My daughter, Mirabai, came and led writing retreats and women's groups. I did a workshop centered on my newly published book, *Fifty and Beyond: New Beginnings in Health and Well-Being*. Every time a group came and spent a week it was if they had blessed the place.

The weavers, too, were beginning to come down to visit us at our home in Bacalar, which was completely different from what they were used to in the

mountains of Oaxaca. They enjoyed being on the water as much as we did and understood the pleasure we took in this part of our lives. It was always a special occasion when the weavers came to visit, although it's been the first generation, our oldest friends, who made the trip.

The second generation is pretty immersed in family life with their own children now growing up and with their increased responsibilities in

Preparing traditional
Oaxacan hot chocolate

the family weaving businesses. And, rather than visit us in another part of Mexico, they come to the United States visiting their various friends and incorporating trips to New York, San Francisco and other cities and tourist destinations.

Their parents have also visited us in northern New Mexico and it's nice that we've had time to share together at our home in Arroyo Hondo, as well as Starr Interiors and that they have had a connection with this part of our lives. It's so much better to experience another's slice of life than only hear about it. The weavers who visit can connect us to our families, our gallery and our environment as well as understand the rhythms of our lives, which, in many ways, aren't so very different from their own.

Florentino Gutierrez and his wife, Eloisa, along with a friend, Hugo, come up to Taos every year at the same time during Wool Festival in October to give a weaving demonstration in our gallery courtyard as well as make the traditional Oaxaca style hot chocolate, which we serve to visitors. We share meals together and our favorite outing is to go to Saturday garage sales, something I introduced them to a number of years ago. They seem to be just as hooked on them as I am. Sharing in the philosophy that recycling is a good thing, for us as well as for the planet, these excursions are always fun. Not having lived in a culture where people throw away perfectly useful things, the idea of the abundance of inexpensive but good used items is a new concept. And being an avid fan of garage sales, I love sharing the experience!

By now Florentino knows to buy the local newspaper and scan the classified section of "The Taos News" looking for garage sales for our annual

Saturday morning excursion. Our visits, always punctuated by a lot of laughter and fun, after several years has become a tradition at Starr Interiors. When we first met Florentino, he was a law student at the university in Oaxaca. He was a talented musician as well as a talented weaver. In the many years that they've been coming up for the Taos Wool Festival, giving weaving demonstrations on the loom (brought up from the village many years earlier), and staying in our guest casita, our relationship has brought us close. No, he never became an *abogado* (lawyer), choosing instead to weave, build a business and a beautiful, spacious home and nurture his children who are now pursuing their own advanced education.

Historic courtyard at Starr Interiors during Taos Wool
Festival. Florentino Gutierrez holding yarn, his wife Eloisa
serving hot chocolate, and Hugo at loom

83

THIRD GENERATION

We were having lunch at Tierra Antigua, the large, airy restaurant built by Pedro and Carina at their new home along the *entrada* when John and I noticed a young woman coming up the path. She veered when she saw that there were people in the restaurant and headed for the side of the house. Edmundo and Alicia, who were there with us, saw that it was their granddaughter and called for her to come and join them. I was not only astounded to see that it was Diana, but that she was in her hospital uniform. What a wave of emotion I felt! From knowing her from the time she was a newborn, to seeing her now in her professional hospital whites, thrilled and moved me as much as if she were my own granddaughter. I really couldn't help the tears that suddenly welled up in my eyes.

Weaver Juan Luis, wife Paula and young son, at the loom
working on an original Line of the Spirit rug

Diana is third generation. I knew her dad, Pedro when he was a small child and then when he and Carina were first married. Now, they were sitting here at their own restaurant in their spacious new house and showroom, watching their oldest daughter return from her day's activities at the hospital. She was on her way to becoming a doctor. I glanced at Edmundo and Alicia and saw the pleasure pass across their faces, proud grandparents. Their warm, welcoming smiles were joyous to see and I felt privileged to have been connected over the years to this special family and to see how their own lives and those of their children and grandchildren have been unfolding.

Every time I see Alicia we embrace long and heartily, as if our being reunited once again is a small miracle. She is my friend in the truest sense of the word. Never would I ever question that friendship. Her love is written in her smile. They welcome their friends and guests with the same generosity of spirit they have passed on to their children and grandchildren, all of whom share that

feeling of genuine happiness and open-heartedness with their visitors.

Their original restaurant, El Descanso, now is firmly established but it's primarily their daughter-in-law Marisela who runs it. Alicia and Edmundo have turned over their large house and the restaurant with its lushly landscaped courtyard to Fidel, their oldest son, and his wife, Marisela. Now they're living close by in a small

Tierra Antigua, restaurant owned by Pedro and Carina Montaño

Opposite: Diana, with parents, Pedro and Carina Montaño. She's just returning from her work at the hospital in Oaxaca in training to become a doctor.
Photo courtesy of author, Susanna Starr

complex they built where they have their own smaller "retirement" house and several other casitas they rent out. Their long years of hard work have diminished, and they can now take the time to quietly enjoy the fruits of their labor.

Fidel Montaño is now in his early forties, an accomplished musician and a fine photographer as well as a weaver. He speaks Zapotec, Spanish, and English fluently, as well as a smattering of other languages. He handles not only his own distinctive weavings, but also those of his father. When we're there, his sisters Antonia or Alicia come over with their own weavings to show us. His wife, Marisela, still looks as lovely and young as she did when I first met her more than twenty years ago. They travel extensively when they can, mostly as a family. Just recently they all returned from an extended visit to New York and Washington, a wonderful experience for the whole family, especially for the teenagers, young Fidel and Sara.

Fidel and Marisela's daughter, Sara, as adorable as her mother, sings along with her father and knows all the words to every one of his songs. Now she's beginning to think of what she wants to study, as she nears the end of high school. She'll have the advantage of being able to pursue whatever she'd like, having gone to private schools in Oaxaca and gaining the opportunity now to develop any area of study she'll choose. She goes to school with Florentino's youngest daughter, Natalia, where both girls are studying nursing. Since they're enrolled in this program, they can easily continue, after their initial studies, on toward other areas of medicine, including dentistry which they're now considering.

Lushly landscaped courtyard at Fidel and Marisela
Montaño's restaurant, El Descanso

Inset: Fidel Montaño in front of his restaurant, El Descanso

The Montaños' second son, Pedro, and his wife Carina live on the property that their parents purchased for them on the *entrada*. With Fidel and Marisela taking over the original family compound and restaurant, Pedro and Carina have started from scratch, building a sumptuous house and showroom as well as a beautiful restaurant. Like the rest of the family, they've always worked hard; now they're working for themselves. Each year has brought the house closer to the completion they've envisioned. In addition to the restaurant and the weaving showroom and space for the looms, they've landscaped the grounds and provided a place to raise farm animals in their spacious grounds at the back of the property. Carina runs their restaurant and for a number of years has run her own small business selling accessories, much the same as her mother-in-law did at the original family compound.

Diana is Alicia and Edmundo's oldest grandchild and her medical school training is a great source of pleasure and inspiration to the family. Her younger brother, Diego plans to spend some time in the U.S. and see what comes up for him as well as developing his English language skills. Like his cousin, Fidel, they are at the age of just getting ready to leave home to pursue university studies, careers, or perhaps entertain new ideas that have not yet occurred to them. Diego, like all of his cousins, is arrestingly handsome. When he and Fidel are together they exude, in a quiet way, a strong awareness of self and a positive attitude toward their future. Alicia, the youngest, also has the quality of noticeable beauty.

Often, at either Fidel's or Pedro's household, the kids would come home from school, sit down, and have something to eat, and then spend time

Marisela and daughter Sara, looking like sisters

together. They are all close friends as well as cousins who share not only common grandparents, but also the entire extended family. Knowing their place in this world has given them a sense of security that isn't always evident in contemporary teenagers in other countries and cultures. Antonia's and Alicia's children, too, all flow easily from one household to another. Far from the sense of alienation that seems to pervade other cultures such as in the U.S., the family members' sense of connectedness is almost visible, like the threads of a web that hold them together.

In Florentino's household, this third generation is well on its way to establishing itself in professional careers. Although he opted not to continue in law school, Florentino has provided the kind of financial security that allowed his oldest son Ricardo the opportunity to go to university and then on to medical school. This handsome young man is now a practicing doctor who some years ago hung up his shingle outside his family home where he sees and treats his patients in his office. It's pretty thrilling to see what all the years of work have done to provide the opportunities that the children of Florentino and Eloisa's are now enjoying. Florentino, deprived of his own parents while still young, is now seeing the flowering that's unfolding with his own children.

Juan, the middle child, is about the same age as young Fidel and Diego Montaño and, indeed, they're friends as well as neighbors, not to mention the fact that their fathers do music together. Like Fidel and Diego, Juan also has embarked upon his own path, studying audio engineering at a technical college in the U.S. It will be interesting to see where the paths of this generation will take them because of the choices that are now available to them. It's definitely a time of transition in the village. Wherever they go and whatever they decide to do, however, it's likely that the strong family ties they have always known and their strong connection to the village and to the traditional ways will continue. Rather than disassociate themselves from ancient rites and celebrations, they seem to hold tight to the richness and importance of their heritage.

Natalia is the youngest of the family, around the same age as Sara and Alicia in the Montaño families. When she celebrated her *quinceanera* (the celebration of her fifteenth birthday), it was a major event. Florentino sent us photos since he and Eloisa had been staying with us just a month earlier, and they knew that we were anxious to hear about it. As in many of the important fiestas that take place, friends, family, and neighbors participated in providing food and music and flowers. It looked like a wedding with hundreds of people in attendance and Natalia and all the other young people in formal attire. These are important celebrations that families take a great deal of pride and pleasure in. Often it's a stretch financially, but they feel the celebration is worth it.

The children of Armando, Juan and young Felipe Gutierrez's children are also friends of these young people. The older children are mostly attending school in Oaxaca where they'll soon decide what they will do for their continuing education.

My own grandchildren correspond in age to those of the Montaño and Gutierrez families. My youngest grandson has now made his first step along his path as a young adult. With them, there's no question of entering into the family business, as the business that has been mine for forty years grew and developed as part of my own specific choice of lifestyles. It has been and continues to be important to me. But their choices will be distinctly their own. They also come from a different culture in that they don't have thousands of years of tradition behind them. They seem to be still strongly connected to their family, but those ties are not from cultural traditions. The likelihood of continuing to live in their community is not nearly as strong as it is with the grandchildren of the Zapotec weavers.

It's wonderful to be able to see this third generation of beautiful young people launched into the world. Some of them will choose to continue in the weaving tradition because they enjoy the way of life it affords. They can work for themselves or work for another member of the same community, rather than work in a more highly structured environment. Many of the young people choose this path.

The weaving tradition of Teotitlan will continue, but the new schools for higher education there, including a college level institution now being planned, will open doors for many more of the families living in the village. It will no longer be necessary for young people to attend private schools in the city of Oaxaca in order to pursue more advanced studies. The new school will provide expanded educational opportunities for this village and the adjacent villages as well.

In the past, young adults from the village sometimes left for the U.S. to find more opportunities to earn money. Invariably they sent money back to their families, although often they formed their own communities in the U.S., actively engaging in life there while still maintaining their own culture. Now young people are finding more opportunities to work close to home,

Zapotec woman selling balloons in Oaxaca zocalo

to be of benefit to their community, and to continue to maintain their traditional culture.

The growing city of Oaxaca, meanwhile, affords even more work situations for the young people of the village. Some have already begun to work in the retail shops started by their family members. These shops have proved to be very successful in selling to tourists who will never make the trip out to the village. Oaxaca has attracted people from other parts of Mexico to live there. In addition, there are many more tourists now from all over the world.

Yet the city still retains its indigenous flavor. Most of the people walking in the *Zocalo* (central plaza) are local people. Many of the women still wear traditional dress. You can identify the *Tehuanas* (women from the Tehuantepec peninsula of Oaxaca) by their long skirts and colorful and intricately embroidered *huipiles* (blouses) anywhere. Frequently there are celebrations and dance performances in the city featuring indigenous people from all seven regions of Oaxaca, as well as other parts of the country. Although tourists most certainly enjoy these performances, they are really for the locals.

Galleries and restaurants in Oaxaca are often Zapotec owned, and this third generation can often find jobs in restaurants (as my own grandchildren have done in the U.S.) or cooking while they're getting started in life or are attending school. Sometimes these are just introductions to life in the city, but they can also lead to careers such as chefs or managers in fine restaurants and hotels.

Meanwhile, local markets continue to flourish. Even with new, modern supermarkets readily available in the city, many folks prefer to shop at their

Danza Folkerico troupe performing outside
of Santa Domingo cathedral

local markets. Anyone who has ever visited Mexico knows the explosion of colors and aromas, and the exciting energy in the markets. The profusion of every kind of fresh fruit and vegetable is a delight to the senses.

Prepared foods have always been found in these markets, allowing anyone with a few pesos to find a good meal at an affordable price. Now, though, many of the markets have become more sophisticated, incorporating irresistible baked goods and great vegetarian dishes in addition to the wonderful, traditional rich Oaxacan fare. There are also special markets, like the Pochote market on Saturdays that features organic foods, coffee, candles, pottery, woven textiles, plants, homemade breads and pastries and pizza as well as traditional Oaxacan dishes.

One Saturday when we were there I was surprised to hear someone call out "Doña Susanna." She was one of the women I've known for many years

Market scene – woman selling produce

Opposite page: Enticing desserts at market; Blind woman selling *chapulines* (fried grasshoppers) at market during season

Woman serving traditional beverages at market

Interior of market showing a variety of produce stands;

from the village, there selling her specially prepared tamales and homemade tortillas. It always feels special to run into people I've known, both from the village as well as from the city.

Yes, Oaxaca has changed but has also retained its sense of place and authenticity. I still love to walk around the Zocalo in the evening although the days of recognizing people seem to be over. Still, the liveliness and sense of *vida (*life*)* remain the same.

Not too long ago, we stayed at a lovely bed and breakfast, Casa de mis Recuerdos, owned by Concha and Moises, the same couple we rented our house from many years ago. It was wonderful being with old friends and visiting the special place they've created in what was originally their family home, with its charming courtyard overflowing with flowering plants and the handmade crafts of the area in evidence everywhere. Of course, the breakfasts, served on beautifully appointed tables, were delicious, carefully prepared, and attractively presented.

Although I've driven the road leading to the village many dozens of times, I still appreciate the beauty of the surrounding mountains. I no longer recognize every house along the *entrada* because there are too many for me to identify now, but there's always a sense of familiarity.

Most importantly, when we step into the homes and showrooms of the weaving families we're most connected with, it's the same as a visit with anyone who has appeared in your life over decades, warm and close and personal. For all the changes that have taken place, this connection is one of the constants.

Fabulous fresh flowers displayed at market

The people I know are happy about their economic success. No one is afraid that their rich, deep culture will be disrupted because of it. They're careful to maintain their language and their customs and have instilled that feeling in their children and grandchildren. Yes, the handmade sandals of their great grandparents have been replaced by store-bought sneakers, and every teenager who can afford one has a cell phone or a tablet. These teenagers are computer savvy and plugged into the same things as teenagers everywhere. But this is not at the expense of the traditional values that have been instilled in them since they were small children.

One of the positive aspects of the changes in village life is in food and drink. Where fiestas used to last for days with an abundance of everything, they've been toned down. Many people have developed a stronger sense of health consciousness and are much more careful about the way they eat. Alicia Montaño knows every good bakery in Oaxaca where they have homemade breads with organic ingredients. Every meal she serves includes fresh salad. Eloisa, too, serves food that is not only marvelously tasty, but healthful as well. As a result, their children and grandchildren have already learned the importance of healthy eating.

This third generation is not only learning all the traditional ways, the language and the rituals that have been part of their culture for thousands of years, but also how to live in and be part of the modern world. Many of them speak, read, and write in English. They understand the Zapotec language of the elders but their everyday language is Spanish, the national language of Mexico. Often this generation is fluent in several languages.

Display of traditional pottery cooking bowls at Pochote market

Although the kids of this generation are ready to go out and explore the world, it's from a strong sense of place, of family, of community and culture. They're not "lost" but excited about their next steps. They're not leaving to "escape" but, rather, to pursue a much broader horizon with expanded opportunities. This is not to say that they will not return to the village, because most of them probably will. However, it will be out of choice not of necessity, a meaningful difference. And, in all likelihood, they'll marry into families within the village. Somehow they're managing to explore the larger world around them, while still maintaining their lifelong connections.

During a recent visit, Fidel and Edmundo invited John and me to what turned out to be an important ceremony that was taking place in the village. Edmundo was about to be sworn in as secretary of the governing committee of the *iglesia* (church), along with the other newly elected committee members. The ceremony was one that had been taking place for many centuries. It was marked by the passing of the *baton* (staff). Like all the other ceremonies I've attended, each step was deeply steeped in tradition.

When we arrived at the church, we congregated in the courtyard outside where a number of people had already arrived. Only one other person there was not Zapotec, but she lived in the village and was, as we were, friends with the Montaños and other families there. At no time did it ever feel that we were intruding. Instead, we were welcomed by various people that I've known for many years.

The women, dressed in colorful embroidered blouses, were already lined up under one of the *portales* (covered part of the patio) where they sat making

Sacred mountain viewed from Teotitlan church courtyard

tejate (a traditional drink made of corn and stirred until foamy). The men, some in traditional straw hats, sat at long wooden tables and benches while the brass band assembled at the other end of the courtyard. Some of the people were seated on a bench under a tree in the center of the courtyard as the newly elected members of the committee readied themselves for the ceremony.

Because it was a serious ceremony, it didn't have the same party atmosphere of other fiesta type gatherings. When the men, led by Edmundo as the committee secretary, filed in they each took their place as Edmundo was handed the *baton*. He received it solemnly, signifying his agreement to accept his responsibilities with honor and dedication to the good of the community.

Afterwards the men passed around cups of the frothy *tejate* and we all drank while the band, mostly horns and trumpets and of course the crashing cymbals, played traditional music. I was pleased to see several of the weavers I knew in the band, including Tomas Mendoza and his now grown son whom I hadn't seen since he was a child. Music has an important role in the village, both the traditional music that Tomas was playing and the more modern band that Florentino and Fidel have formed. In fact, some of the teenagers are thinking about going to the U.S. to study music as their next step after high school.

While we were there, we noted the original thousands of years-old glyphs on stones carved by the ancient Zapotec that were incorporated into the walls. The Spanish had built the church over the existing Zapotec temple more than

Edmundo Montaño standing at church column after
being sworn in as committee chairman

Women from the village preparing *tejate* (traditional drink) to be served after swearing-in ceremony, while Edmundo's granddaughter, Sara looks on

Committee members drinking the celebratory *tejate* at table

Tomas Mendoza and his son playing in the band celebrating
Edmundo's swearing-in at the *iglesia* (church)

Ancient Zapotec glyphs on original columns stuccoed over by the Spanish
when they built the present church

five hundred years ago. Although many of the families are Catholic, there is a strong sense of identity and connection to the ancient religions and customs of their ancestors, a constant reminder of the ways of their people, practiced for millennia. Seeing these original designs carved into the stone walls is always thrilling because many of them inspire the designs still being used in the weavings they produce today.

And what are my own grandchildren, kids who are pretty much the same age as those in the families we've been connected with, doing at this point in time? My oldest granddaughter is living in the state of Washington, where she moved a few years ago with her children. They may have made this their new home. This is a pretty common occurrence in the U.S., families relocating to areas away from their parents, forging a new life for themselves and their children. I've been fortunate in that my two daughters have remained living in Taos, affording me that special pleasure of seeing my grandchildren grow up.

My oldest grandson is a rehab counselor. Living in California for the past few years he, too, has found his place, doing something meaningful to him and to the young men he works with. He plans to attend college to continue in his chosen field. His younger brother has moved to Albuquerque, New Mexico. It's not yet apparent what will unfold for him. It's likely that he'll find his place somewhere other than the small town of Taos where he and his older brother have been raised. The potential of a more expanded life and different opportunities encourage young people to make their own way, often in different geographic locations.

Although my grandchildren have a very real attachment to their parents and immediate family, they don't have the long history of tradition that their counterparts in the village have. Nor do they have the same expectations of continuing in the steps of their parents or grandparents. They've all been encouraged to make their own decisions about their lives but unlike the kids from the village, this doesn't necessarily include the understanding that they will return to the life that they knew growing up.

Not all who have left the village feel that same tug to return. For many who have settled in the U.S. and who now have kids of their own, going to school and becoming part of the new community has become their new life. However, most have simply taken their village life with them, celebrating fiestas in the same traditional ways they always knew. Although the kids are part of the American culture and way of life, they still keep their connections to their community, much as people who have immigrated from other countries and cultures traditionally have. They take in the newly arrived and maintain the integrity of their culture while still participating and being part of the larger society.

When Juan, who is the middle child of Florentino and Eloisa, attends college in the U.S. he'll stay with his mother's family who have been settled in southern California for a long time. He'll be surrounded by aunts, uncles, cousins, and others of the extended family and community, so the transition to living in another country and culture for a while should be relatively easy. The same, of course, holds true for any of the teenagers who will make the decision to live in the U.S. either to study or to visit. They won't have to go out hunting for an apartment in an area where they know no one. Instead, they'll have love and attention and lots of help from the community.

The main thing that sets this third generation apart from previous ones is that the changes that have taken place over the past forty years have greatly expanded their vistas. They now have many more choices. What they will do with this explosion of possibilities remains to be seen. Life in the village, though, is likely to continue in the state of gradual change that's been taking place over these three generations.

I am no longer working with Abi who, after twenty years of being together during the time she was director of the Line of the Spirit, has decided to shift her life visions and now has a café she's started at her home in Oaxaca. But, when we're there, she works with us as she always has, taking us to the village daily and spending time with Alta Gracia and her son, Jacinto (Jazy), who has taken Abi's place as art director of the Line of the Spirit production. Jazy, who was a child when I first knew him, now has young children of his own. He over-sees all of the production of the Line of the Spirit and confers on a daily basis with Alta Gracia, his mother and original dye maker.

Alta Gracia has been working on the project since its inception, and her continuing work as dye maker has been one of the most important founda-tions of this designer collection. Now, working with her son who has become the art director, their home has become the base of operations for the production. With their proximity to the adjacent river that goes by their property, Alta has indulged herself, over the years, in creating beautiful gardens. As gardening is one of the loves of my life, too, every visit finds me

Dye-maker Alta Gracia standing in her garden with
newly dyed skeins of wool

touring her amazing collection of trees and flowers. Her roses, and there are many, seem larger and more fragrant than any I have known and the fruit from her various trees, more luscious.

In addition to her being a dye maker of extraordinary talent and a first-class gardener, she also prepares food for fiestas and, just as a sideline, makes her own chocolate to sell. We both now have gray in our hair and more lines in our faces, but we're both still passionately involved in this art project known as the Line of the Spirit. Our families are now grown and Alta has the pleasure of having her grandchildren live with her, able to share these precious years of growing up. She's lost her husband, Don Pedro, but with her expanding family and her ongoing interests, she has adjusted to these later years of her life and her own personal changes. The beauty in her smile and the wisdom reflected in her face are testimony to a life well lived.

I love visiting there, being together with Abi again, talking and discussing designs and colors with Jazy and his mother, Alta. Eating the sweet fruit of the trees, seeing what pieces are being worked on at their looms, and simply dropping in on their lives are important parts of any visit to the village. When I think of being there, the scene is always bathed in sunlight, the air always filled with perfume, and skeins of brilliantly dyed yarn are hanging on the walls.

Line of the Spirit *equipo* (team), Alta Gracia, Jacinto and Abi

Opposite page: One of the original Line of the Spirit weavers,
Jovita Mendoza, standing in her *tienda*, one of her
other successful business enterprises

Maria Bautista works with her daughter, Isabel,
on spinning dyed yarn into skeins

Ascencion Martinez sitting in her patio
with outdoor kitchen in background

Top row from left: Florentino Gutierrez weaves with his brilliantly dyed yarns;
Accomplished Line of the Spirit Weaver, Valentino Mendoza at loom

Bottom row from left: Alta Gracia's husband, don Pedro, working on large Line of the Spirit
weaving; Line of the Spirit original design, Navajo Inspired, weaving in process on the loom;

Top row from left: Valentino's wife, Anita working on "Sacred Symbols" for Line of the Spirit;
Efren Lazaro works on one of his signature red pieces, while father, Braulio, looks on

Bottom row from left: Jovita Mendoza at loom with family and Mito Martinez (at left) looking on;
Tomas Mendoza at loom working on his original design

CONCLUSION

In celebrating forty years of working with the group of Zapotec weavers in the village, I have built a business and made enduring friends. They, too, have built businesses and have provided increased employment for other weavers. Taos is a lot different than the way it was when we began our interwoven odyssey and so is the village, although both locations retain the same sense of "place" as they did. When we're in the village, the people I've known are familiar to me, our relationship old and established. When I'm in Taos, although it's grown also, I can still count on running into old friends in markets and restaurants.

It's this sense of intimacy that is the defining term to describe these forty years. It spills over to customers and clients in the gallery as well. Knowing that these weavings are now finding their place in someone's home, where they will be seen, used, and appreciated completes a circle. I know the weaver and now have met the new owner. There is nothing impersonal about it. In my heart, and I hope in the minds of the buyers as well, I'm very aware that the purchases represent part of weavers' lives.

Accomplished weaver Felipe Lazaro plays
his instrument while his wife looks on

My own children lived through some challenging years in this home that, at the time of their growing up, was basically unfinished. The house was cold, Ramon and I were gone during the winter months on our excursions to Mexico and they were left with whoever we could find who would live at the house with them. They had to often fend for themselves in trying to arrange transportation to visit friends. It was difficult and they made many sacrifices. Their own children, however, this third generation, did not have to deal with those kinds of challenges and their lives, growing up, were a lot more comfortable, just as their counterparts in Teotitlan.

Although, at the time we did not consider them to be sacrifices, we too lived a life that was different from the middle class lives we had previously known. On our early buying trips we spent close to our last dollars from our meager funds on purchasing rugs, leaving us with little left for the drive back home. On one memorable return we ate *bolillos* (French bread rolls) with tomatoes and avocados for virtually the entire trip. That was the same trip we sold our car jack for enough money to cross the border.

But those days marked the beginning of building a business that started out with trust as its foundation. Without knowing us, weavers gave us their work on partial payment and partial credit. It was the only way it could have worked. We didn't have money to buy enough to have any kind of meaningful inventory to begin a new business and they didn't have a way of marketing and distributing their work. None of us had a five-year plan, a projected trajectory of sales, a market analysis or any experience, other than the weavers' expertise in producing rugs and wall hangings and our enthusiasm and dedication. I believe that it was because of our intention and that of the weavers with the important and essential element of trust that enabled this business to grow to where it is today, enabling all of us to enjoy a richer and more comfortable way of life for ourselves and our families.

When Florentino and Eloisa and Hugo come to visit, I love hearing the *comentarios* (observations) about the village as it is now. There are changes that have taken place that have affected the way this village has afforded opportunities unknown to any of us when we began forty years ago.

The place of women has changed dramatically. They now participate in committees such as school and medical clinics, where once only men served. But the property changes are truly significant. Where once division and ownership of property was automatically passed on to sons, now daughters are included as well. The meaning is obvious. Women have achieved an opportunity to be independent financially and socially as well. They can now have recourse as to where they can live rather than assuming that they would marry and move to their husband's home.

The *primaria* (elementary school) has been augmented by the *secundaria* (middle school) since 1975 and the *preporatoria* (high school). Now the plans for the new university are under way, expanding educational opportunities for some of the less affluent villagers. Utility services, such as electricity and water, have reached the areas where the less affluent or newly beginning families live.

As for me, I've earned my living doing something that is my passion. Although I've set about trying to disengage from the everyday demands of being in the gallery, as long as the front gate is open, it will always lure me in. I've been fortunate enough to have as our sales director for many years, Leah Sobol, who has taken over all the myriad tasks of running the gallery as well as being director of sales. My daughter Amy continues our family involvement by running the office. Their help has given me the time and space to gradually withdraw.

This is as it should be. I'm now at an age where that kind of everyday presence is no longer necessary. I am still in touch with the weavers on a regular basis and, of course, see them on our visits to the village. I've been very blessed in this business that has unfolded for me and with each person that I've been connected with, both in Taos and Oaxaca.

Unlike many people who have managed to earn livings by taking money out of Mexico, I've been fortunate enough to have been able to put much of it back into Mexico, by creating Rancho Encantado. Although it's been passed to someone else who shares the same feeling about it as we have had, we still have our home there on the beautiful waters of Laguna Bacalar. That home not only has enabled me to continue an important part of my life, but has provided me with the chance to rest, renew and restore. Ramon, who has his home next door to us, lives there full time.

I can and do spend time doing nothing but looking out at the water, listening to the birdsong and checking out the new blossoms. Each morning, on my daily walk, I gather my *tulipanes* (hibiscus) and other flowers and leaves, bring them back to the house and arrange them in every room. Instead of the Zapotec way of having them placed on the altar, every room has its own arrangement of fresh flowers, celebrating life and beauty.

During the many decades of raising children and working to build a business and a home, there was never much time left to read, write, garden, or paint. But now those building years are over for me and for many of the original weavers I started working with. We haven't withdrawn entirely, but we're well on our way. Although reading still feels like an indulgence, when I'm in the warm, tropical sunshine with no other demands, I can spend many hours of every day catching up on and immersing myself in reading. Winter months spent in the Yucatan have also provided a beautiful space in which to write.

Having divided my everyday life into various parts has enabled me to escape the grip of the dominant U.S. culture. It's allowed me to be exposed to other cultures over a long period of time and to forge bonds of enduring friendship with other peoples. It's also given me insights into the relatively new way of life here in the U.S. in contrast to the ancient tribal way of life of the indigenous people of Mexico.

So far, the weaving families of the village have managed to appreciate and afford many of the things that this new age of electronic communications can offer, as well as things we take for granted, such as refrigeration, cars and trucks, and good roads. But, thankfully, their sense of tradition remains intact. They still honor the elders in their community and women are not left alone to fend for themselves in isolation when they have no spouse with whom to share the raising of their children.

Fiestas and religious celebrations continue to provide the cohesion that keeps the village intact. Producing weavings is an important part of what they do. But the pursuit of financial success is a dividend rather than the driving force in their lives. Having an altar in each home is a reminder of their connection to and their sense of the spiritual, which infuses all that they do. Most important for me is seeing their commitment not only to their own families, but also to their community and to the preservation of their culture.

Their elected officials serve without pay so self-aggrandizement or personal profit are never their goals. A person is not judged by the number of TVs he owns or the kind of vehicles she drives, but how they comport themselves. Being a person of honor is more of a distinguishing attribute than being "ambitious," which, in their usage, describes someone who wants to get ahead at the expense of others.

In all my years of working with some of the families of this village, I have never observed the sense of alienation and isolation that I see regularly in the U.S. I'm sure there are many factors that contribute to this, the strong family connection being one of them. However, in all fairness, they have not really been offered the kinds of opportunities that have existed in the U.S. during the twentieth century. Now that they are part of the twenty-first century in the same way as many westernized countries, perhaps there will be some shifts. But I don't see major changes on the horizon and I'm happy for that.

Just as the official before him passed the baton to Edmundo Montaño or to Florentino Gutierrez, I will pass a symbolic baton to the next person who takes my place. But I will always be grateful for these years, celebrating the many experiences, holding the many memories, and treasuring the deep and enduring friendships.

One of the gallery showrooms at Starr
Interiors, Taos, New Mexico

ACKNOWLEDGMENTS

My thanks to: Bobbi Shapiro who heard the first read-through of the manuscript, adding her own astute insights and observations. Bonnie Lee Black for editing the first draft of the manuscript; Marlan Warren for her immense help, dedication and suggestions for getting the final book ready for launching and post publication promotion; Melody Swan for her talent and enthusiasm for putting the book together in her artistic way; Winn Kalmon who not only went over each word with her experienced eye, but whose friendship has been so meaningful to me; Leah Sobol whose love for and dedication to Starr Interiors has allowed me the time, free of any gallery concern, to work on this book knowing that the gallery would be run under her watchful eye; Florentino and Eloisa Gutierrez for their stories about the village

Author, Susanna Starr, at Starr Interiors in Taos, New Mexico and their close, warm and continuing friendship; Edmundo and Alicia, Fidel and Marisela, Pedro and Carina and all the Montaño family for their enduring and deep friendship; Felipe Gutierrez, Armando, Juan and Felipe (jr.) for their trust and confidence through the years; Efren Lazo for his warm smile. The incomparable Alta Gracia for the years spent making the Line of the Spirit collection what it is and for all her family, Jose, Faustino and especially Jacinto who has spent these last few years as the guiding hand in the production; To all of the weavers involved with the Line of the Spirit production, especially Jovita and Valentino Mendoza, Felipe Lazaro and his wife, the talented Eliseo and Maria Bautista and their daughter, and Juan Luis, Paula and their sons; Abigail Zarate for the years of working together as director of the Line of the Spirit production and her close and caring personal friendship; Harriet Martin, whose enthusiasm is a constant reminder of our old and meaningful connection; Mitzi Linn for her ongoing friendship and helpful observations; Judie Fein and Paul Ross for the wonderful and fun week we spent together in the village while they were filming Zapotec Weavers: A Love Story; Ramon Childers for reading the manuscript and making helpful suggestions and relating important anecdotes based on his own first hand shared experiences; Most of all to my family, Mirabai Starr, Amy Starr and Roy Starr for their ongoing endorsement and enthusiastic support of all I do; to my partner and co-creator of this book, John Lamkin, for all the many hours of locating key photographs, dealing with all the technical aspects and being there throughout the birthing; And, to the memory of Freddi Gutierrez from Teotitlan.

Susanna Starr, Author

Susanna Starr is an entrepreneur, photographer, speaker, artist and travel writer. She is the owner of Starr Interiors in Taos, New Mexico, which began as La Unica Cosa in 1974. She is also owner, designer and director of the acclaimed designer weaving collection, Line of the Spirit. Susanna lives in Northern New Mexico and Mexico and has had over twenty years experience in the hospitality business as owner of Rancho Encantado, an eco-resort and spa in Mexico. Her degree in philosophy is from the State University of New York at Stony Brook. She is International Food, Wine &

Susanna Starr

Travel Writers Association (IFWTWA) Regional Membership Coordinator for Riviera Maya & Oaxaca, Mexico. Susanna Starr is also the author of FIFTY AND BEYOND: New Beginnings in Health and Well-Being published by Paloma Blanca Press. Her articles have appeared in numerous publications, including Soul of Travel Magazine, The Examiner, Let Life In, and the award-winning travel journal, Your Life Is a Trip. Her website is www.SusannaStarr.com.

John Lamkin, Photographer

John Lamkin is an award-winning journalist and photographer based in Taos, New Mexico and Mexico. He is a board member and Global Membership Chair of International Food, Wine & Travel Writers Association (IFWTWA). Lamkin attended the San Francisco Art Institute and founded San Francisco Camerawork. In addition to food, wine and travel writing, he has worn many hats in public relations, copy writing, technical writing, and poetry. He is the former editor of Camerawork Quarterly and Music of the Spheres Magazine, and a member of the North American Travel Journalists Association (NATJA).

John Lamkin

In addition to his freelance work, John is a contributing writer for Luxury Latin America, Luxury Avenue Magazine, The Examiner, Reuters America, Suite101, Your Life Is A Trip, and Jetsetter. He is fluent in Spanish. His website is www.TravelWritingAndPhotography.com.

CPSIA information can be obtained
at www.ICGtesting.com
Printed in the USA
LVIC04n2116060714
393120LV00003B/9